THE FARM

David Kherdian

THE FARM

by David Kherdian

Introduction by Brother Jeremy

TWO RIVERS PRESS / *Aurora, Oregon*

I would like to thank the editors of *A Journal of Our Time*, *The Armenian Post*, *Encore* and *Tigris & Euphrates*, a special issue of *X*, a journal of the arts, for first publishing some of these poems.

Copyright © 1978 by David Kherdian. All rights reserved. No part of this book may be reproduced or transmitted in any form or by any means, electronic or mechanical, including photocopying, recording or by any information storage and retrieval system, without permission in writing from the Publisher.

10 9 8 7 6 5 4 3 2 1

ISBN: 0-89756-001-9
Library of Congress Catalog Card Number: 79-64355

TO MY FAMILY

David Kherdian lives just fifteen miles down the road from where my monastery is. I have known him now for several years. When we met, each was told that the other was a poet. Soon we were speaking so compatibly about what we thought poetry is, we were expressing a similar joy about the sounds of our language, and we were tracing this agreement back to what we identified as its sources. These sources—very different at first glance—have much in common; and exposing them here can, I hope, serve as a fitting introduction to *The Farm* poems.

Every person has a point of view. When a poet has his, it is from there that he writes his poems. The point for *The Farm* poems is Kherdian's experience in the Gurdjieff Work. Not many may know what this might mean. I didn't until I had met David. But the farm, to which these poems refer, is a place where over a hundred people meet regularly to study and practice living by the teachings of Mr. Gurdjieff. To be brief about the Gurdjieff Work and about my own Benedictine monastery is to be unfair to both, but being brief anyway: one of the things that each comes down to is providing its members with an atmosphere and a disciplined way of life in which they can be present to the present. The present is the only moment we have. It is not the only moment that is important; it is simply the only moment that we have. It is from there that we feel the facts of our past and the pull of the future. Ours, then, is an effort to trust the present, to look there for the encounter with Mystery.

David Kherdian is someone who never gets wrapped up in his poems. This is because he knows that a poet is someone who has access to a world that isn't really of his making. Instead, a poet is someone who will use words to show how Mystery unveils herself in some event or moment. An artist can forget this, thinking that he has made or at least discovered whatever it is that the work expresses. Then you are wrapped up in what has been made instead of in the Mystery which you sensed and sought to reach toward. But this sort of individualism is not the point of existence. We are in this together. Talent may coalesce around this or that person, but it is an energy bigger and more than any individual, and it remains in the world to coalesce elsewhere long after an individual is gone.

Kherdian is also a poet who knows that a certain ambiguity is the poet's gift to the reader. Not just any ambiguity, of course, or then anyone would be a poet. But his are often poems that will rub along a certain edge, you don't know what it is, but here are words whose coming forth provides a breakthrough more deeply into present things. They are poems which provide a solution to nothing. But then we are not looking for solutions anyway. They do hold us fast to a dimension of existence that we might not otherwise manage to stay near.

All of this about David Kherdian could be said before *The Farm* poems. The question with any new collection is can you still say it, can you say it more, do you need to say something new. Well, yes to all three. There is something the same here and something new.

In the introduction to David's first book, *On the Death of My Father and Other Poems*, William Saroyan suggests that here is a collection of some very excellent poems but with a few that try too hard. Concerning the poems that try too hard, Saroyan said, "This suggests that the poet is traveling, and finding out where he's going as he goes." David's subsequent books mark these travels, a journey, I would suggest, more and more toward The Farm, more toward present things, more toward community. Something gradually emerges in these collections which perhaps might be called a sacramental principle. Everyday awareness has two points. For example, I (1) see a bird (2). But sacramental awareness has three points: I (1) see a bird (2) and in the seeing I see Mystery (3).

The Farm contains poems in which the experience of community life in the Gurdjieff Work is what Kherdian is seeing. Facts about this way of life occur in the poems, and it helps to know that this is so. There is talk about a meeting and movements hall, a main house, a school, work week, the women and the men and the children. These are places and events in the life of the community, and it is in this life where another dimension uncovers itself, and the poet is there with words as it happens.

A number of these poems are about work, and in these I find a special resonance with the monastic life. Like monks, people in the Gurdjieff Work find in labor one of the main places for the breakthrough of Mystery. There is something so utterly factual about work that if mystery occurs there, then its appearance can be trusted as human and true. Here is an encounter beyond all telling expressed in a phrase from "The Farm" that monks would like very much: "the music and mysticism of the work/concealed in our hearts."

Though all of the poems somehow have this Gurdjieff environment as their occasion, they are not poems which belong only to those who study his teaching. For these are poems simply about living where and how you are. And seeing it. Perhaps two poems especially might show the Gurdjieff connection with this. "Sunday Before Easter" is a poem in which the poet is distracted, where the poetry itself almost breaks apart expressing the distraction. But its recovery is the calmer knowing that a place has been found "where not knowing has a place." "Celebrating Gurdjieff's One Hundredth" shows that even with all this technology, ours is still a world that can be experienced as sacred. We can still pray. We still come. We still affirm. We still move in processions.

—Brother Jeremy Driscoll, O.S.B.
monk of Mount Angel Abbey

CONTENTS

epigraph
Sunday, Early, 5
The Farm, 6
The Main House, 7
Cattadoris, 8
As I Approach the Farm on
   the Last Day of November,
   1977, I See, 9
Early Sunday, 10
Winter Prayer (1), 12
Winter Prayer (2), 14
I Ride the Red Tractor, 15
I Ride the Red Tractor, 18
She is weeding in the far corner, 19
Waiting, 20
Mary Jane, 22
Crows, 23
Sunday Before Easter, 24
Dear Children, 26
In the Greenhouse, 28

On Seeing for the First Time
   the Picking of Flowers for
   the Meeting Room Table, 29
Easter Morning, 30
Easter Evening, 32
Weeding, 33
Amidst the talk, 35
The Dance, 36
To the Man or Woman who
   Brought their Meditation
   Cushion to the Top of the
   Barn and Left it there,
   allowing Me to Imagine
   Your Vanished but Living
   Presence an Hour or Two Later
   When I Came to do My Work, 37
Strangers in a Distant Land, 39
Oregon/Winter/My Tree, 40
Mulching, 41
Renee, 42
Celebrating Gurdjieff's One Hundredth, 45

THE FARM

*In the great firmament
the eternal world spins on—*

*The summer pear blossoms
will make a perfect mat
for the autumn frost—*

*The days slow to a crawl
or speed past quicker
than the heart can follow—*

*Still, all the stars are present
if one will only look up.
Now and then, with right timing,
I catch them
casting their white nets
of light
against the indigo night.*

Sunday, Early

The dog called Bear
is sleeping in front
of the frosty kitchen doors,
where the misty cooks
are breathing their steam
into the bread that rises
with their breath
to the dining hall above

where one of us, myself,
lazily looks out the window
to see the dog called Jessie
running weed-high and happy,
to bring the first untested news
of the early Sunday day.

The Farm

Looking out from the window
  top of the barn—

The wet, burnished green
  and empty fields—

The summer days come back
  in a flush—
  work week, its color and climate of talk—

I quietly return to the
  Indian corn
  the working men
  the women's voices drifting up—

Together we are bringing in the sheaves
  the music and mysticism of the work
  concealed in our hearts

The Main House

They are laboring now on the living room
    of the main house—men
    sturdy, quietly at their work:

The peaks and valleys of their sizes
    make a form in which a humming
    can be heard—

The women, just beyond, are carrying
    mortar, bricks and trowels
To an herb and rock garden
    that is slowly
    taking hold—

They are beautiful
    in their plainness
    in their devotion to rocks and plants—
They look up from their bricks at the men:

They cannot help themselves
    they smile
They are women in need of men.

Where they are a tiny flower has
    bloomed—
the chimney is going up

Cattadoris

Sometimes, out of the corner
   of my eye
   I see him bobbing
   in reflections of glass
Atop the greenhouse
   or under—
   flashing the foundation
   or leading the frames
Getting the sections to fit
   and groove and flesh.
Or just walking silently
   to the workshop and back
   on his own worn path,
Drawing his face up when greeted
   to endure the pain that
   precedes each uttered word.
Something very small and quiet
   and deserving our love
   is making something very big—
   pane by pane—go up.

As I Approach The Farm on the Last Day of November, 1977, I See

Something new—
   wood neatly piled
   in double rows before
   the school—which is also
Something new—
   and where Nonny inside
   is teaching puppet making
   to the children—who are,
   of their kind, Mrs. Staveley
   tells me
Also something new—
   is the world become then
Something new—
   Toddy has just disappeared
   with a pan of new dough
   into a very old hearth—
To make it new, make it new.

Early Sunday

It is the sight of a woman
   feeding chickens
   that causes a man to
   remember again what
   came to him once
   long before words
   long before the first written poem
For in seeing her there
   he knows again all form
   all motion,
   and the rhythm and sequence
   of time:
But the lugubrious poet must write.
   He must write because,
   being a man who wishes words
   to accompany living time
   he will have his poem—
   and so he writes:
The early morning maid
   on the farm
   with dew in her hair
   and a bowl in her circling arm

> *is throwing seeds*
> *in nets of spray*
> *to the chickens*
> *that have gathered round.*

When the scene becomes the absence
   of the scene it was
   and only its ambience remains
He quietly walks to the hen house
   to see there dainty in
   a feminine hand:

> *shhh baby chicks inside*
>   **QUIET PLEASE**

There is a beauty in all this
   beyond the telling

Winter Prayer (1)

By the road in winter
   the golden stubble in hatfuls
   of broken life
   rests:

The pheasant rises, flaps,
   floats into the
   slumbering green
   of that only field:

One looks for days, for
   months, at the same
   scene—a desert of
   likeness, a boredom
   of years—

If nature doesn't remind
   us, guide us, how
   will we awaken
   to the hour—

There is a pheasant of
   trouble of hope—
   a bundle of colored stars
   in your funny crown—

As hard to extract
   to hold and shake free
   as it would to rumble
   that field there—where
   the pheasant flew a moment ago—
   and make him all fall down
   gasping, into your
      openmind

Winter Prayer (2)

I think I will go now
   to the withered winter garden
And breathe a single summer memory
   into just one pale and slumbering leaf

That when it next awakens
   it may turn to all the others
   and say:
   The life of man was awake
while we slept—

It has prayed and we are its reminder
   that their prayer was answered
   and must be prayed again.

I Ride the Red Tractor

I ride the red tractor
   a stranger to this green earth,
   these turbulent, thundering skies—

Strapped to the seat
   I am the whirling hub
   of this musical sphere;
   the weight of my buttocks
   moor me helplessly, while I
   quiver in anticipation and fear.

Am I the host of machinery
   or the captive of something
   I cannot understand;
   vaguely, only vaguely knowing
   that nature has tamed this instrument
   I think I command.

The starlings arrive
   to greet their tractor friend.
   As we jog along, they jump and then
   fly ahead.
I witness the turning up
   of grubs and worms,
   the life this damp earth
   secretly defends.

We are moving now in figure 8s
   the tractor and I,
   performing a perfected ritual
   I am taken along to see.

There is a life of earth
   I have tried to deny,
   helplessly now I enjoy its muscled strength
   its beckoning call.

Waiting for her love to be answered
   she quietly breathes in and breathes out
   all time.

It awaits, it endures, it survives
   our careless wants—
its truth so immense it holds aeons
   in a breath
gathers and shakes loose a multitude
   with the flick of its cloddy hand—
still hoping its final embrace
   will   not   be
    an   earth   cancelling   hug

I Ride the Red Tractor

I ride the red tractor
   across the green earth
The host of starlings
   who purple come
Fearless at last of this
   human form—
And we are suddenly arm-extended,
   wing-beat abreast,
And suspended, joyous, I am being
   churned across the earth—
The far-flung hope of some distant hand.

O if I could only be to bird and animal
   red tractor or green
And come with them at will
   across this vibrant, mysterious land
Rejoicing in the food
   revealed by each turning tread
And they secure in the halo of my love—
   this is all I would of holiness be,
And to the rhythm of wing-beat
   and animal tread we would move
Across the golden face of day,
   into the rosy back of night.

She is weeding in the far corner

She is weeding in the far corner
    of a field.
Know her by a single tool
    used for going deep
    a paper bag
and clothes that know no season.

It is her work that takes
    her there—
she calls those weeds her enemies.
    Reader, you cannot know what this means.
    It is a paradox perhaps.
But we who love her best
    we think we understand.

Waiting

for Don Hoyt

It was quiet at dusk
   when we arrived—
Movements had been delayed—
   an extra passenger, a missed plane—

Waiting, I carried water to the
   greenhouse plants
from the pump just beyond—
   and saw a movement
in the grass—a pheasant
   as still as us
   as watchful, waiting—

While some weeded
   others talked—
slowly others turned in the kitchen
   preparing tea—

In such quiet as this
   one knew the film
   of atmosphere would hold—
We took our measure
   and its own—
it was ours but it was not
   for us alone—

And then we ascended the stairs
   and waited
   in the stillness
each to each

Mary Jane

Thank you for being there
munching on grass—
beside the new school

with your young pudding face
your nose full of flies—
and your funny little horns

it is right that you are there
just there—
on your pallet of straw

where you greet the children
each morning—
as they arrive

it is almost as if you were never away
your moo the moon the new month of April—
opening our eyes to all the possibilities of love

Crows

A tree of crows
   make a Crow Tree
and across the new green field
   a Field of Crows.
I turn around, and astonished,
   see a great new body of crows
   spring from that opposite field
   into the open, sunny air—

crows crows crows crows crows
   I repeat with my tongue, swallowing
   black:
and turn this time to my work, amazed,
   wondering how to put
such play, such unpredictable
   humor
into my own daily life.

Sunday Before Easter

Against the newly painted
   movements hall—
   during the luncheon discussion—
new, tiny,
   black and busy flies
had congregated in the air
   where they buzzed
   and chased themselves
   in circles—
and, with every 3rd or 4th sweep
   of the open-air circle
   their lives or activity had taken,
one of them (they were all doing this
   of course) would
   rush at another
   frantically, seemingly angrily—
   though they never actually touched or met.

I forgot everything
   for a moment—
   my intention in being there,
   my aim, my desire
   to be present

   (was I present after all)—
and admired this scene that was
   beyond my comprehension.
In truth, I suppose, it wasn't
   that exciting,
   but it *was* something—
   something different, as my
   mother would say—
and I felt a certain helpless pleasure
   in knowing, really knowing,
   that I don't understand anything,
   not *especially* flies buzzing,
   not *only* flies buzzing,
   but *anything, everything*!
I just don't know!

Then I turned back
   to the other mortals
   in the room—and listened
   to some of their buzzing—
grateful to be in a room
   where not knowing has a place—
   a very big place
as big a place as wanting to know.

Dear Children

Let me write a poem about a hide-out
   as real and even more poem-like
   than any of those I knew and
   inhabited once.
Of all the sights on The Farm
   your hide-out is the most amusing,
   the most profound—because made of
   nothing real (of money earned and
   spent—material bought and/or
   bargained for) it is outside
   the karma of harm.
You made its bumping carefree shape
   with the free imagination itself—
   and being free of loss it is therefore
   also free of time.
It reminds me of the imperishable
   in ourselves—the children we too
   must once again become.
We are far more awkward going down
   than you are coming up;
   and we never could have fumbled
   anything like this together ourselves—

so forgive us for understanding it
so well, and for never having once
mentioned it to you or to ourselves.
If we pass your hide-out by, time after
time, unnoticing, you at least
should not be fooled.

In the Greenhouse
   for Nonny

In the seeds in her
   hands
all memory of life and growth and
   death
is held in whirling motion—
and now
   as her cupped hands move
   she begins to feel the canopy
   of Heaven turn above her shoulder
while slowly she tucks her tiny
   stars of remembrance
back into the earth from whence
   they have come—
feeling their burnished thoughts
   bloom in her head

**On Seeing for the First Time
the Picking of Flowers for
the Meeting Room Table**

She had been softly picking
flowers of weeds
among the trees in the orchard grass—

and as she stood and held
them from her
with arms outstretched—

I imagined their million seeds
spilling over her hand
and making a trail of stars—

that would follow her
as she began to walk
with her flowers—

that were becoming the bouquet
becoming the jewels
that ornament our meeting room nights.

Easter Morning

The absolute stillness of 6 A.M.
Only the smoke rising from the barn
where the women are preparing breakfast.
The grey clouds are again themselves,
but they move with such quiet at this hour
that only they know they are there.
The sun is far away
and we feel far away from the sun.
The blackbirds that have been with us
for so long now
that they are a part of us
just flew in a cluster
into and out of my sight.
They are a comfort and will fill
a small wound.
I am told the children will hunt
for Easter eggs after breakfast.
That is good. I do not know what
it means but it is good.
While new ceremonies are being born
old ones are quietly dying out.

Soon the cars will be arriving
and with them the wings of other voices,
but now it is quiet, unearthly quiet,
only the swift and intermittent black
birds, the clouds like smoke, and
the smoke an earthly cloud.
The day of death may not be unlike
this moment now—when one is helplessly
alone and glad to be, unable not to be ready
for the entrance of the next experience,
which may be the last, or only the last
of its kind.
I have to remember that it is Easter
and try to realize again what that means.

Easter Evening

You look up and the trees are all at once green.
It takes all day to stop and look
and then suddenly the sky is all its one color:
clear, in that color that is no color,
the color of quiet evening—
the evening color of the sky in spring:
and there, far off on the wide horizon,
is a rosy glow, the glow of evening,
the rosy substance of spring;
and below that, at the point
from which this poem and remembrance begins,
are the green leaves that have suddenly
come home to summer;
the occasion of the lives of trees
having begun
exactly and as always
perfectly to the beat of celestial time/
and earthly time/
reminding us, now at Easter,
what it means for us
to make our own lives.

Weeding

Weeding, I see all the night flowers
   of day—
the shaded twisted specimens of lost needs.

Not wanting them, still they come—
   bending to pick them
   they resist my demand.

All seed, all flower, all bloom
   and fade away—
but so tiny some of them, that
   only from not needing them it seems—
   not wanting them—do they come.

But now at once they are revealed to the eye
   that must go to their level
   to pluck them out.

We are here, they whisper, you are there:
   you must concern yourself to decide:
and now and then a tiny blue and white
   streaked flower,

   as pretty as anything the eye
   has ever seen
appears among the thorns and thistles
   and grasses endlessly rooted.
All these too must go!

This is the pain of choice.
   The responsibility to be assumed.
For even if we were to gather and save
   the few attractive flowers they give:
   in one day, two days, maybe three
   they would also fade
        and die.

Amidst the talk

Amidst the talk
   the many noises
the clatter and important strife—
   whether on the stairs
   in the kitchen
the bay or the barn—

   always she comes with broom
and pan
   unnoticed, utterly silent
   keeping this chosen work
and welcoming the room   the berth
   that others allow.

Quietly the quiet color
   of her life   our life
   goes on—

in another country, Armenia,
   strangers were welcomed by
   the washing of feet.
You, perhaps alone, will know
   what that means.

The Dance

The women are gathered
    about the filbert trees
sitting in clusters of
        shadow and light
    in the early October green.

When they leave with full baskets
    under their arms
the men that follow
    stop and puzzle over pressed grasses
and the forms that vanished presences
    leave,
suddenly still
       to feelings
    unnamed   unknown

To the Man or Woman who Brought Their Meditation Cushion to the Top of the Barn and Left it There, Allowing Me to Imagine Your Vanished but Living Presence an Hour or Two Later When I Came to do My Work

Thank you, I used it
while shelling corn—
leaving it where I
last sat during the
actualization of my work.

When you found it Monday
and returned to your spot,
did you feel the work I
put into it the day before,
and did you wonder to yourself
if I felt the work
you had left in it all the mornings before that?

We want to touch everything
in this manner, with all
the parts of our bodies, consciously,
with all our feelings and thoughts,
deliberately,
for it is in this way
that we are trying to
awaken to The Farm
as heart

Strangers in a Distant Land

As I lean on my shovel
 close of day
sun glints under stones
 under eaves,
and disappears into gray
 brooding skies—

the lost eerie cry of the peacock
 announces (is it time? is it the
 setting sun gathering her children home?)
 that she has seen again her ugly feet—

I slowly turn back again
 against wood and field and home
understanding the loneliness
 of beautiful women

Oregon/ Winter/ My Tree

The bark like a cocoon
is storing the water
of the endless rains
into its many sky-running
downy canoes—
until, at last,
they butterfly green become
a tropical forest
of endless soft-mossy
mountains
and crevices wet—

and now the sun
for a moment
has made it all shine
emerald green, purple,
and muted brown-black,
until I am so over-
whelmed by its
beauty
that I must turn
and make something of my own
in verse

this poem

Mulching

For Jeff and Dick

In the rain-quiet gold and green of winter
    two men in rubber wraps
    spread spoiled hay
    under the orchard trees,
the piled bales slowly dissolving
    under their work—
and there, proudly squatting,
    old Blue considers the barnyard rooster
    (who has strayed here) and
    wonders if this is territory fit to protect—
while the rooster dreams of distant hens:
    and in the tension between them
    the question hangs:
while silently the work of the men
    goes on.

Renee

I visit the little school
   warm my chilled back
   against the hot wood stove,
   and sit on a far cushion,
   hoping not to be seen—
And watch the scene unfold,
   naturally, in its easy,
   every day way—
And slowly, one by one, they
   come and show me what
   they do, and ask that
   I button their smocks
Or they just tell me their
   names, and ask me mine.
One of the teachers' names is
   Judy, the other is Mr. Smyth,
   for everyone here
   has taken the name
   they wish to be called by—
There is Gottlieb, Erin and Vance;
   Tasha and Kirsten and Matt;

Alfred and Aubrey and Leo;
   to mention only a few.
Finally, the pixie of the crowd—
   always, every gathering of souls
   must have one that is the most
   vivacious of the lot—
Comes and jumps into my arms,
   unconcerned over the restraint
   and caution and quiet that
   contains the rest—
You are my outdoor elevator,
   I tell her—which floor
   shall it be—but she only
   giggles and falls backwards,
   while I hang onto her knees—
This one used to be Mona,
   Mr. Smyth says, but she
   decided to be reborn, and
   that's what her new name means—
That's right, that's right,
   formerly Mona says,
   my name is Renee.
Maybe, I think, the school itself
   should have been called that:
   it seems that kind of place.

When the time comes to leave
   I ease out the way I came, unnoticed,
   knowing something,
   something very precious,
   has been kept alive.

Celebrating Gurdjieff's One Hundredth

January 13, 1978   *Aurora, Oregon*

The fog lifts, falls,
    is penetrated by invading
    lights of cars.

I imagine candles in procession
    walkers in Asian mountains,
    chanting as they come to prayers.

Here their descendents arrive
    in shields of tin and glass
    over mended gravel roads.

O brothers, our Fathers
    in the distant firmament,
    with our drum the silent wheel
    that turns
    and our prayer beads rattling
    in the engine
    that hums under the hood

    We   Affirming   Come